Suaviter dormi, lupe parve

Schlaf gut, kleiner Wolf

Liber bilinguis pictus

Ulrich Renz · Barbara Brinkmann

Suaviter dormi, lupe parve

Schlaf gut, kleiner Wolf

Translatio:

Palle Rolfs (Lingua latina)

Audio and Video:

www.sefa-bilingual.com/bonus

Password for free access:

Lingua latina: **Sorry, audio or video is not yet available in this language.**

Lingua Theodisca: **LWDE1314**

We are currently working on making as many of our bilingual books as possible available to you as audio books and videos. We kindly ask for your patience if there is no audio or video version in your language yet! You can keep up with the progress of our work on our website:
www.sefa-bilingual.com/languages

Noctem bonam, Tim! Cras quaerere pergemus.
Bene dormi!

Gute Nacht, Tim! Wir suchen morgen weiter.
Jetzt schlaf schön!

Foris iam tenebrae sunt.

Draußen ist es schon dunkel.

Quid Tim facit?

Was macht Tim denn da?

Foris ad campum lusorium it.

Quid ibi quaerit?

Er geht raus, zum Spielplatz.

Was sucht er da?

Lupum parvum!

Sine quo dormire non potest.

Den kleinen Wolf!

Ohne den kann er nicht schlafen.

Quis advenit?

Wer kommt denn da?

Maria! Pilam suam quaerit.

Marie! Die sucht ihren Ball.

Quid Tobi quaerit?

Und was sucht Tobi?

Machinam fossariam suam!

Seinen Bagger.

Quid Nala quaerit?

Und was sucht Nala?

Pupam suam!

Ihre Puppe.

Nonne liberi ad lectum ire debent?

Feles valde miratur.

Müssen die Kinder nicht ins Bett?

Die Katze wundert sich sehr.

Quis nunc advenit?

Wer kommt denn jetzt?

Mater paterque Timis.

Sine Time dormire non possunt.

Die Mama und der Papa von Tim!

Ohne ihren Tim können sie nicht schlafen.

Etiam plures veniunt! Pater Mariae.

Avus Tobii et mater Nalae.

Und da kommen noch mehr! Der Papa von Marie.

Der Opa von Tobi. Und die Mama von Nala.

Cito ad lectum!

Jetzt aber schnell ins Bett!

Noctem bonam, Tim!

Cras nos quaerere opus non est.

Gute Nacht, Tim!

Morgen müssen wir nicht mehr suchen.

Suaviter dormi, lupe parve!

Schlaf gut, kleiner Wolf!

The authors

Ulrich Renz was born in Stuttgart, Germany, in 1960. After studying French literature in Paris he graduated from medical school in Lübeck and worked as head of a scientific publishing company. He is now a writer of non-fiction books as well as children's fiction books.

www.ulrichrenz.de

Barbara Brinkmann was born in Munich in 1969 and grew up in the foothills of the Bavarian Alps. She studied architecture in Munich and is currently a research associate in the Department of Architecture at the Technical University of Munich. She also works as a freelance graphic designer, illustrator, and author.

www.bcbrinkmann.de

Do you like drawing?

Here are the pictures from the story to color in:

www.sefa-bilingual.com/coloring

Enjoy!

The Wild Swans

Adapted from a fairy tale by Hans Christian Andersen

▶ Reading age: 4 and up

'The Wild Swans' by Hans Christian Andersen is, with good reason, one of the world's most popular fairy tales. In its timeless form it addresses the issues out of which human dramas are made: fear, bravery, love, betrayal, separation and reunion.

Available in your languages?

www.sefa-bilingual.com/languages

My Most Beautiful Dream

▶ Reading age: 2-3 and up

Lulu can't fall asleep. All her cuddly toys are dreaming already – the shark, the elephant, the little mouse, the dragon, the kangaroo, and the lion cub. Even the bear has trouble keeping his eyes open...

Hey bear, will you take me along into your dream?

Thus begins a journey for Lulu that leads her through the dreams of her cuddly toys – and finally to her own most beautiful dream.

Available in your languages?

www.sefa-bilingual.com/languages

Special thanks for his IT support to our son, Paul Bödeker, Freiburg, Germany

ISBN: 9783739952017